‘We’ll Get
in the Long Grass!’

Jim Brown,
Commemorative Booklet
to Celebrate 100 Years of the
Enniskillen Unite Branch (TGWU),
1923-2023

Jim Quinn

Umiskin Press

November 2023

Paperback ISBN 978-1-7391564-7-3
Hardback ISBN 978-1-7391564-8-0

In Memoriam

Frank Buckley represented Labour in Dundrum on Dublin/Dún Laoghaire/Rathdown County Councils and was honoured by the Party's Larkin Thirst for Justice Award in 2012 for his role in exposing corruption as Council Group Leader. A long-standing and respected member of the Party's Administrative Council, he twice contested Dublin South in 1981 and 1982. He died on 2 September 2023.

Marilyn Hyndman, a lifelong campaigner for social justice, was a film maker who co-founded Belfast Arts Lab and Northern Visions TV. She published *Further Afield: Journeys from a Protestant Past* (Beyond the Pale Publications, 1996) relating the experiences of working class Protestants and contributed 'Like mother, like daughter: Sadie Menzies, 1914-1996, & Edwina Stewart, 1934-' to *Left Lives in Twentieth Century Ireland – Communist Lives*, (Umiskin Press, 2020). She died on 22 January 2022.

Dermot Keogh began his working life as a journalist before studying in Dublin and Florence. His *The Rise of the Irish Working Class: The Dublin Trade Union Movement & Labour Leadership, 1890-1914*, (1982) was a pioneering work. When he died on 6 September 2023, he was Professor of History and Emeritus Jean Monnet Professor of European Integration Studies at University College Cork.

Flor O'Mahony, born in Dalkey, 1946, was a Labour Councillor in Dún Laoghaire, 1967-1974; served as Adviser to Labour Leaders Brendan Corish, 1973-1977, and Frank Cluskey, 1977-1981; was elected to the Seanad Administrative Panel, 1981-1987; and served as MEP for Dublin, 1983-1984. He was unsuccessful in Dáil elections and became a public affairs consultant. He died on 28 July 2023.

Frank 'Frankie' O'Neill worked in Áras an Uachtaráin and was a member of SIPTU's Dublin District Council and National Retired Members' Committee. He died on 22 July 2023.

Bride Rosney, a school principal and Executive member, Teachers' Union of Ireland, was Special Adviser to President Mary Robinson, 1990-1997, and RTÉ Director of Communications, 2001-2009. She died on 22 September 2022.

Frank Sherry, a percussionist, served on the Executive of the Irish Federation of Musicians & Associated Professions, 1976-1991, the last ten years as Treasurer. A Labour Party activist in the 1950s/1960s, he worked in Guinness and played in a variety of bands and orchestras. Born in 1928, he died on 6 January 2023, aged ninety-four.

Sally Shovelin, born in in 1957 in Rathmullan, County Donegal, graduated in social science from University College Dublin and worked for the Eastern Health Board/HSE and as Community Development Officer in the Department of Social Protection. She campaigned for Republican prisoners in Long Kesh and Armagh Jail, for women's rights and the LGBT community. From 1988-1991, she was seconded to the Local Government & Public Services Union (now Fórsa). She died on 4 August 2023.

Jim Brown – Working Class Hero

Foreword from Owen Reidy, ICTU General Secretary

Jim Quinn has valiantly strived to recover Fermanagh labour's past – and will continue to do so. His 'Labouring on the margins - trade union activity in Enniskillen, 1917-1923' appeared in *Saothar 15*, 1990, and grew into *Labouring Beside Lough Erne: A Study of the Fermanagh Labour Movement, 1826-1932*, published by Umiskin Press in 2019. This was a ground-breaking study of labour's industrial, political and social experience in a provincial town. Quinn also contributed ''No homes for people or books': labour's housing struggle in Enniskillen, 1915-1932' in Seán Byers & Francis Devine, *William Walker 1870-1918: Belfast Labour Unionist Centenary Essays,* again published by *Umiskin Press* in 2018.

This body of work remains unique and his study of Jim Brown both adds to it and heralds the imminent appearance of a second volume that will bring Fermanagh's labour story from the 1930s to the 1970s and a third volume that will conclude in the present. The combination of all these works has importance not just for labour historians and contemporary activists but for those interested in any aspect of Lakeland County history.

Quinn's researches demonstrate that Fermanagh workers' experience of struggle is markedly different to that of those in large urban and industrialised centres like Belfast, Cork, Derry or Dublin. As someone reared in Donegal with strong family and organisational connections with Derry, I recognise much of the landscape in which Fermanagh workers operated and the obstacles they faced. Some problems were, of course, common to workers across Northern Ireland – sectarian and gender divisions, unemployment and job insecurity, the absence of effective political representation of workers' needs within the workplace or community. Such problems were, however, exacerbated by Fermanagh's relative isolation, the institutionalised neglect of communities west of the Bann, and the insularity of local class structures. For Jim Brown, the road was stoney and steep.

What emerges, however, is the courage and generosity of spirit among the county's working class activists with no better example than Jim Brown. His union – and that of Quinn – was and is the (Amalgamated) Transport & General Workers' Union, now Unite, and it is appropriate that this pamphlet celebrates the Enniskillen Branch Centenary.

The pamphlet also befits the work emerging from the Unite History Project - www.unitetheunion.org/who-we-are/history/unite-history-project/. Developing 'history from below', the Project has involved hundreds of activists in recovering their past in order to inform their future, an exercise not in antiquarianism but contemporary organisation. The Project will produce six volumes that are to be highly recommended, not least for their accessibility of writing and style, the case studies and questions they pose to the reader, and the generation of pride in achievement installed in members.

The most recent publication – *Unite History Volume 5 (1974-1992) – The TGWU From Zenith to Nadir?* – contains a chapter co-ordinated by John Foster, 'Ireland: working for class unity in extreme circumstances', that examines the union's central role in challenging workplace sectarianism, promoting gender equality, challenging division and opposing public sector cuts. It is recommended to all trade unionists of whatever union in Northern Ireland as, to quote Foster's concluding remarks,

> 'In all this, the radical traditions of the ATGWU ... continued to play a vital role – an understanding of the class politics, the need to challenge an exploitative system as argued by Connolly and Tom Mann, played an essential part in building the wider unity needed for effective trade union struggle.'

The comments are pure Jim Brown. Quinn contributed significantly to the construction of Foster's chapter, together with other key Fermanagh ATGWU activists Tommy Campbell – now with the union in Aberdeen – and Davy Kettyles through their relating of their own experiences of organisation and activity. The Unite History Project catalogues much of the ATGWU's significant contribution to the Irish movement, recognised in the number of ICTU Presidents the union provided – Norman Kennedy, 1961, a key figure in Congress's reunification in 1959; Matt Merrigan, 1985; John Freeman, 1995-1997; and Eugene McGlone, 2011-2013. In addition, Congress Presidents were drawn from what are now

Unite Heritage Unions: Andy Barr (Sheet Metal Workers), 1975; James Morrow, 1960, James Graham, 1984, and Jimmy Blair, 1990 (Amalgamated Union of Engineering Workers); and Brendan Mackin (Amicus), 2003-2005.

Jim Brown kept the trade union and labour tradition alive in Fermanagh for both urban and rural workers during some very difficult periods from the 1950s to the Millennium. He held Labour's flag aloft through the Red Scare period and maintained cross-community unity through the years of conflict in Northern Ireland, a difficult and at times stressful process. It was not merely a personal crusade as Brown saw the need to develop and encourage a new generation of activists to follow his legacy of militant trade unionism and socialist politics. Finally, he ensured that the activities and issues of Fermanagh workers were kept in the eyeline of leaders in Belfast, Dublin and London, and constantly reinforced the message of the value of a united movement throughout the island of Ireland. As the former ICTU Assistant General Secretary based in Belfast, I can understand what it took for Brown to maintain the stands he took and can see the dividend that allowed our movement to stand firm against division, violence and repression and to maintain our optimism and belief that we can effect progressive change for working class people, whatever the odds.

Reading Jim Quinn's study of Brown, I am reminded of how significant – and largely unheralded – his own contribution to class struggle has been. Active in his union since 1978, he worked for Counteract, Congress's anti-intimidation unit, before heading Unite's Organising Academy in London until his retirement in 2016.

'Retirement' is of course a misleading term for people like Jim Quinn as he continues his life-time commitment to his class as Secretary of Fermanagh Council of Trade Unions leading campaigns on social issues, opposing public sector cuts and, through cultural and other events – not least his writings – constantly striving to galvanise class consciousness in his home county. I salute his contribution and value the paths he has beaten for younger people like me to follow and learn from. It was a road familiar as Jim Quinn followed in Jim Brown's footsteps.

Reading this pamphlet, I understand what an inspiring mentor Jim Brown was for Jim Quinn and his fellow 'cubs'. Brown's life story is informative and inspiring, an ordinary man making an extraordinary contribution with most of those who benefited from his activities utterly unaware of him. Brown was not after recognition or praise, however, and undoubtedly could have chosen a smoother path in life.

I strongly recommend Jim Quinn's pamphlet and congratulate him for shining a light on a local working class hero. I sincerely hope that any who read it recognise that their obligation, having done so, is to apply its lessons, to write the next chapter in the work Jim Brown dedicated his life to.

Owen Reidy addressing ILHS 50th Anniversary Second International Conference, Visions of Labour & Class in Ireland & Europe, Liberty Hall, September 2023

Bench honouring Jim Brown in Brook Park, Enniskillen

100 Years of T&G/Unite the Union in Fermanagh

The current Enniskillen Branch of Unite originates from the oldest Transport & General Workers' Union (TGWU, T&G) branch in Fermanagh which was founded in 1923 at a meeting in the Labour Hall, Townhall Street, Enniskillen. There were two other branches in the county, one based in the English Sewing Cotton factory and a general branch in Lisnaskea covering a range of workers from that side of the county. Several of the heritage unions of Unite then had branches in Fermanagh: the Amalgamated Engineering Union (AEU) Branch Secretary was William Henderson from Lisbellaw, and the Union of Construction, Allied Trades & Technicians (UCATT) – in 1923, the Amalgamated Society of Woodworkers – Branch Secretary was Jack Hoey from Derrychara in Enniskillen. More will be written about their activities in the second volume of the history of Fermanagh's labour movement to be published in 2024.

The five Branch Secretaries who have kept the T&G/Unite Branch alive in the county over the last one hundred years are saluted here.

John Jones – 1923-1931, was active in the Tyneside-based National Amalgamated Union of Labour (NAUL) from 1918 and lived in Corporation Street, Enniskillen. He had been a boot cleaner in the Royal Hotel prior to becoming T&G Branch Secretary. He served as a Labour Councillor on Enniskillen Urban Council with William Kelly.

John Jones (Junior) – 1931-1937, ran the Branch after his father's death and later became a prominent bookmaker in the town.

James (Jas) Bradley – 1937-1949, had been active for several years in the town and was recorded in 1918 questioning election candidates about their position on Suffrage and Labour rights. He was employed as a porter when he was a young man and later worked in the

Insurance Industry. He served as a Labour Councillor on Enniskillen Urban Council for more than twenty years.

Jim (James) Brown – 1949-2003, was a T&G member in the carting firm of Wordies when he became Branch Secretary and the longest serving in that position.

Derek Parton – 2003-to the present – has been a Library Service driver with the local Education Service for many years and has been Branch Secretary for two decades to date and a delegate to Fermanagh Council of Trade Unions. He has been involved in many campaigns around health and education services over the years.

Sadie Nevin (Coleraine T&G), Jim Brown, Jim Quinn & Carol Nevin with Enniskillen Branch Banner which she designed and painted, Mayday 1985, Belfast

Contents

Jim Brown & Jim Quinn with striking Nottinghamshire miner, Bill Chapman, at a fund raiser in Enniskillen during the 1984-1985 Miners' Strike.

Acknowledgements

We would like to acknowledge the assistance of a range of people in the production of this booklet. Francis Devine of the Irish Labour History Society, a good friend to the Fermanagh labour movement, encouraged us to record and publish our local labour and trade union history. He has been particularly helpful in editing this publication. Mervyn Hall, a member of the Fermanagh Genealogy Centre and a volunteer with Enniskillen Castle Military Museum, helped us uncover Jim Brown's Army records from World War Two. The members of the Old Lisbellaw History Group provided some of the illustrations in this publication and other information on Jim Brown and his family connections in Lisbellaw. Old Enniskillen and Benny Cassidy, whose library of old Fermanagh pictures continues to be an important resource for local history researchers, gave valued assistance. Enniskillen Library allowed us to monopolise their newspaper archives during the research for this booklet and their helpful, courteous and always cheerful staff were vital to the project's research. Ken Ramsey related the story of his father who knew Jim as a young man, carting goods from the Enniskillen Railway Station prior to its closure in 1957. The late Marilyn Hyndman, who interviewed Jim Brown in 1996 for her book *Further Afield: Journeys from a Protestant Past*, provided a useful reference of Brown's life and kindly gave permission for its use in any commemoration of his life. The Ireland Regional Committee of Unite the Union made a substantial financial contribution toward the costs of production and the Fermanagh Branch of Unite the Union also made a generous subvention. Finally, Jack Mc Ginley of Umiskin Press and Christy Hammond of CRM Design & Print, who have both strong trade union ethics, produced an extremely high-quality publication.

Jim Quinn,

Enniskillen, September 2023

Acronyms

ACE	Action for Community Employment
ATGWU	Amalgamated Transport & General Workers' Union
CPI	Communist Party of Ireland
ECDP	Enniskillen Community Development Project
ERC	Enniskillen Rural Council
FCRA	Fermanagh Civil Rights Association
FCTU	Fermanagh Council of Trade Unions
FTUC	Fermanagh Trades Union Council
ICTU	Irish Congress of Trade Unions
ITUC	Irish Trade Union Congress
NIC-ICTU	Northern Ireland Committee – Irish Congress of Trade Unions
NICRA	Northern Ireland Civil Rights Association
NILP	Northern Ireland Labour Party
NIWC	Northern Ireland Women's Coalition
NUAAW	National Union of Agricultural & Allied Workers
PD	People's Democracy
PUP	Progressive Unionist Party
RUC	Royal Ulster Constabulary
T&G	Transport & General (TGWU)
TGWU	Transport & General Workers' Union
TUC	Trades Union Congress

Umiskin Press, Ireland

Umiskin Press is a not-for-profit publishing house, publishing commissioned and non-commissioned works mainly, though not exclusively, works of labour history, Labour interest, trade union issues, poetry and cultural matters. Umiskin is a townland in Kilcar, County Donegal, birthplace of the McGinleys.

Dr. Kieran Jack McGinley is the Principal behind Umiskin Press having previously been the Chairman of Watchword Ltd. Umiskin's recent publications were two volume of ***Left Lives in Twentieth Century Ireland*** co-edited by McGinley and Francis Devine (October 2017/April 2019);(Sean Byers and Francis Devine's ***William Walker Centenary Essays*** (October 2018) and Mike Mecham's ***William Walker Social Activist & Belfast Labourist 1870-1918*** (October 2019).

Recent titles from Umiskin are Toni McManus's biography of ***T J O'Connell***; Devine & Mac Bhloscaidh's ***Bread not Profits*** and Callan & Desmond's ***Labour in Dun Laoghaire Rathdown 1919-1999***

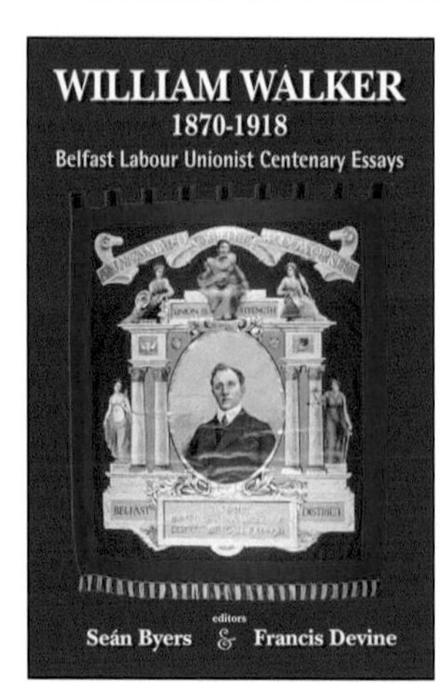

We'll Get Them In The Long Grass!

The Life of Jim Brown

Rural Communist – Trade Union Leader – War Veteran – anti-Fascist

James 'Jim' Brown was born on 18 June 1924 in Brook Street in the village of Lisbellaw in Fermanagh about six miles from the county town of Enniskillen. Lisbellaw (Lios Béal Átha – Ring Fort at the mouth of the Ford) is a small village beside Bellisle, the former seat of the Mac Manus clan where the *Annals of Ulster* were written.[1] The most prominent industry outside of farming in the 1920s was the Lisbellaw Woollen Mills set up in 1858 and remaining in operation until 1968. [2]

Brook Street in Lisbellaw where Brown was born in 1924 (photograph courtesy of Old Lisbellaw member)

Brown died on the 17 June 2003 in his Housing Executive home in Creamery Park, Lisbellaw, where he lived with his wife Margaret. He was the youngest of four children born to Elizabeth Brown (née Bowles), a domestic servant, who married John Brown, a serving soldier in the 11th Battalion of the Inniskilling Fusiliers on 4 June 1915. Their first child, Adeline was born on the 24 March 1916. A son William was born on 15 of August 1918 but sadly died of influenza at six months old on 1 March 1919, possibly a victim of the 'Spanish Flu' epidemic. Another daughter, Georgina, was born on 23 February 1920.

Early Years

Jim Brown related some of his childhood experiences to the late Marlyn Hyndman for her book *Further Afield, Journeys from a Protestant Past*:[3] 'We were very poor, my father pulled out at some stage of the journey and my mother worked as a scrubber night and day to make a couple of bob to rear us'. Brown parted with religion very early in life and related the following story to Hyndman:

> 'My mother used to make sure we went to Sunday School at the Church of Ireland. If you attended all year for the length of Sundays, you got going to Bundoran (a local seaside resort). Now I had missed a couple of Sundays, but the teacher gave me the ticket anyway. We were set down in a big shed in Bundoran to have our meal and on the table in front of us were two Paris buns and a cup of tea. That would have cost no more than one and a half pence in those days. The clergyman came around counting and he looked at me and said, 'You didn't go to Sunday School for the qualified period' – which is true; I hadn't – 'You're not entitled to this' and he took the two Paris buns and the tea away from me. I had to starve for the rest of the day because I had no money. That finished me with the church. I'll tell you what age I was; I was nine, and that finished me.'[4]

Brown left school at twelve years of age and was hired out to local farmers for six months at a time. He told how some farmers provided decent food and accommodation while others did not. Some tried to create a dispute with the hired worker towards the end of their term so that they could withhold payment. Blair's study of hiring fairs supports Brown's story of being hired at twelve, noting that that Hiring Fairs were held In Lisbellaw twice a year into the 1930s.[5]

Brown's War

Brown joined up on 29 January 1940, aged fifteen and a half. He falsified his date of birth as 18 June 1919 when in fact he was born on the 18 June 1924. Brown was big for his age standing at 5'10" and weighing 149lbs. He described himself as a general labourer in the enlistment papers, working as a Quarryman with Edward Dolan in Lisbellaw for £2 a week. He initially signed up with the Royal Inniskilling Fusiliers and his recruitment officer was Captain J.P. Wray. At the start of World War One, Captain J.P. Wray, Drumcoo, Enniskillen, was appointed Recruiting Officer for the Enniskillen area. In 1914 he joined up and led to the Recruiting Office a large body of the National Volunteers. They were posted to the Inniskillings in the 16th Irish Division. Later, Wray went to Africa and served in one of the Crown Colony regiments there. He was very seriously wounded. Wray was the son of the late J.F. Wray, formerly a well-known solicitor in Enniskillen, a Royal Scholar of Portora, and, before his death, Secretary to Fermanagh County Council, and for a period Chairman of the Enniskillen Urban Council.[6]

Brown was posted to Omagh Barracks for training on 10 June 1940 and was transferred to the 10th Battalion of the Cameronians. It seems that there was some family connection to the Cameronians which prompted him to seek a transfer. By 2 March 1941, Brown is described in army papers as a Rifleman in the 10th (Lanarkshire) Battalion, The Cameronians, (Scottish Rifles). He transferred again in February 1943 to the Seaforth Highlanders and went on to fight in the North African Campaign. In 1944, he took part in the Normandy invasion and the later Battle of Europe. In August 1944 he was wounded in action (his second injury). He was awarded the Africa Star with 8th Army Clasp in December 1944 (AFB 2063) and the 1939-1945, Italy, France, and Germany Star Defence Medal. Brown like many of those who experienced the horrors of war rarely spoke about his experiences, but he did relate a story on the 50th Anniversary of the D-Day Landings. He was moving up the beach under heavy fire when his friend took a direct hit from a shell and was essentially vaporised. We can only speculate as to the affect such an experience had on a twenty-year-old but in Brown's case it manifested itself in a life-long opposition to violence. He was often quoted the saying, 'An eye for an eye leaves everyone blind'.

Hyndman relates his disillusionment with a system in which he saw himself, his sisters and his mother living in slum conditions with no running water or other basic amenities but nonetheless compelled to pay the poor rates. His political awakening began when he found a copy in the trenches of *The Ragged Trousered Philanthropists*, the socialist classic and semi-autobiographical novel written by Irish housepainter and sign writer, Robert Noonan who wrote under the pen-name Robert Tressell.[7] Brown recalled reading through the book several times during breaks in the fighting and thinking 'That's me!'. He went on to read books by Jack London the American novelist, journalist and activist and the *Communist*

Manifesto by Karl Marx and Frederick Engels.[8] Brown also remembered his friendship with a radical Scottish Lieutenant Sinclair who condemned Churchill for not opening a Second Front in 1942 and played 'The Red Flag' on the piano in an old tent at the end of a day's fighting.

Brown was placed in the 11th Holding Battalion in February 1945 and officially demobbed on 20 November 1945. One of his final acts before leaving the Army was to challenge a charge of being AWOL (Absent Without Leave) against him in 1945. Like many young soldiers, he had been brought up on charges a few times during the war. His challenge was successful and his final Army papers recorded him as being of good character. Brown had fought and won the first of many battles for fairness.

Demobbed to Bristol and Back To Fermanagh

For Brown, as one war ended, a new one began on the streets of Bristol where he joined the T&G. He met veteran Belfast Communist Betty Sinclair in the People's Bookshop which she ran in Bristol's Upper Maudlin Street and began selling the *Daily Worker* and *Irish Democrat* on the city's streets.[9] He remained in Bristol until 1948 when his mother became unwell in Lisbellaw and he returned home.

Shortly after returning, Brown obtained work as a carter for Wordie's who had the contract for transporting various produce by horse and cart between Enniskillen Railway Station and local businesses such as the Scottish Wholesale Co-operative Society stores and factory on the Sligo

Workers outside the Scottish Wholesale Co-Operative factory on the Sligo Road, Enniskillen, date unknown (photograph courtesy of Fermanagh County Museum)

Road. Coincidentally, he ended up living beside the son of one of those who mentored him in Wordie's, a man called John William Ramsey who had also faced being ostracised by the local establishment because he refused to toe the line. Ramsey was also a staunch, if more reserved, local trade unionist.

Jim Brown and Margaret Elliott on their wedding day, 1948

On his return, Brown met and married his soul mate, Margaret Elliot, with whom he spent the rest his life in Creamery Park, Lisbellaw. Margaret's brother John also lived with them.

Serving the The T&G

By 1950 Brown had become the lay Secretary of the local branch of the Amalgamated Transport & General Workers' Union (ATGWU), the Irish title for the London-based Transport Union, better known as the T&G in Northern Ireland.[10] The Branch was established in the town in January 1923.[11] Brown replaced the long-time Secretary James Bradley who was also a Northern Ireland Labour Party (NILP) Councillor. Bradley had largely retired from trade unionism and local politics when a revival of the anti-Partition movement in Enniskillen's North Ward in 1948 led to him losing his Council seat because of the NILP's position on Partition at the time. When the Irish Free State (Saorstát Éireann) declared itself a Republic in 1949, the Labour Government in London responded with the Ireland Act guaranteeing the constitutional position of Northern Ireland. The Irish Trade Union Congress (ITUC) condemned this move but it was snubbed by the British Trades Union Congress (TUC) and ultimately the NILP was pushed to accept Partition.[12]

One of Brown's early achievements was to organise the local Woollen Mills of Henderson & Eadie in his home village of Lisbellaw. Several workers from the mill had been victimised for organising just after the First World War and an attempt to organise again in 1943 led to the victimisation of five workers. Their treatment was raised in the Stormont Parliament by the Armagh NILP MP Paddy Agnew who was born in Donagh, a small village between Lisnaskea and Newtownbutler. Agnew called for the establishment of a Trade Board for the woollen industry. This was refused by the Minister for Labour, John Fawcett Gordon, who said four of the men left voluntarily and one was dismissed for refusing to carry out instructions.[13] Brown told Hyndman how he put one hundred membership forms into the mill through a contact and succeeded in signing up ninety-eight workers. On 20 March 1954, the local paper announced that the woollen mill workers had been organised and obtained wage increases of between 4s 6d and 7s 6d per week.[14] In an unrelated act but one worth recording, Brown had saved the life of a twelve-year-old boy who had been leaning out the window of a speeding excursion train from Bundoran to Enniskillen. When the door of the carriage flew open, Brown's swift action in grabbing the boys' clothes and pulling him back into the train undoubtedly saved his life.[15]

Information about Brown's activities in the 1950s remains scarce. It was the infamous 'Red Scare' period when workers with communist beliefs were excluded from union positions. It was a difficult period for Labour in Northern Ireland with no seats being won in Stormont elections between 1949 and 1958. Indeed, they won no parliamentary seats outside of Belfast except for Paddy Agnew in Armagh in 1938.[16]

Brown related being at a meeting in Dublin in the 1950s when he came across a demonstration against unemployment which involved blocking O'Connell Bridge with bicycles and a sit-down protest. He joined in the protest and the chanting. His accent was picked up by a large Garda involved in clearing the protesters who told him in no uncertain terms how he would send him back to the North and what he would do with him if he returned. This undoubtedly refers to the frequent protests organised by the Dublin Unemployed Men's Association in the early 1950s. The sit-down protest was novel at the time and provoked a strong reaction and in August 1953 there was a conflict with Garda and several leaders of the Unemployed were arrested.[17] Clearly Brown's socialism knew no parochial or geographical boundaries.

In 1962, Brown was elected to the ATGWU Irish Regional Committee, the ruling body of his union in Ireland. He held that elected position until 1989. With the demise of the railways in Fermanagh in 1957, he moved jobs to the Electricity Board as a linesman and later in the same role to Post Office

Post Office Engineering Union pickets, Enniskillen, 1969: l-r P.J. Leonard, Jim Brown, Fred Simpson, Mervyn Hassard, Jim Moore, Percy Rankin & Robert Evans

Telephones (now BT) where he remained until retirement. Although Brown joined the Post Office Engineering Union (POEU) and was on the picket line in July 1969 with his work mates demanding a pay rise,[18] his first interest remained his organising work in the T&G where he was continuously re-elected as Branch Secretary.

In February 1964, Brown attended a lecture in Enniskillen Town Hall about socialism. The lecture was one of a series organised by the St Michael's Old Boy's Union. St Michael's was the local Catholic Grammar School. The guest speaker on the night was a teacher in St Michael's, Colm Gillespie, an Armagh man and one of the founding members of the Fermanagh Civil Rights Association (FCRA). In February 1969 representing Enniskillen along with Bill Barbour, Jim Lunny, and Dr Robert Simpson, the Protestant Chair of FCRA for a period. Gillespie published a booklet, *Fermanagh Facts*, showing the levels of unfairness and discrimination in the county. He resigned for a period from FCRA along with the Chairperson Robert Simpson and several others in protest at its domination by the People's Democracy grouping.[19] Gillespie, a local schoolteacher, was also a member of the Fermanagh Labour Party earlier in the 1960s. He died suddenly in 1979.[20]

At the lecture, the local predominantly nationalist paper, the *Fermanagh Herald*, remarked specifically on Brown's reference to others at the meeting as 'brother'. During the meeting, he queried a situation in Enniskillen Rural Council (ERC) where Nationalist councillors were not prepared to supply protective clothing in the form of gloves to dustmen to protect against dermatitis and it took the intervention of some Unionist Councillors to have them issued.[21] Brown was referring to the response from a Nationalist Councillor on ERC, J. Regan from Belcoo, to the letter from the union when he said, 'Next they will be wanting umbrellas!'[22]

Baptist Gamble Stands for Labour

In October 1964, Brown seconded the NILP Candidate in that year's Stormont election, Baptist Gamble from Treel, Boho. Gamble was a progressive farmer from the Boho area. Although Gamble was unsuccessful in the election, Brown related a story where he claimed that the local Orange Lodge in Lisbellaw initiated an enquiry because it was believed Gamble received several hundred votes in the village because of 'Brown's' influence.[23]

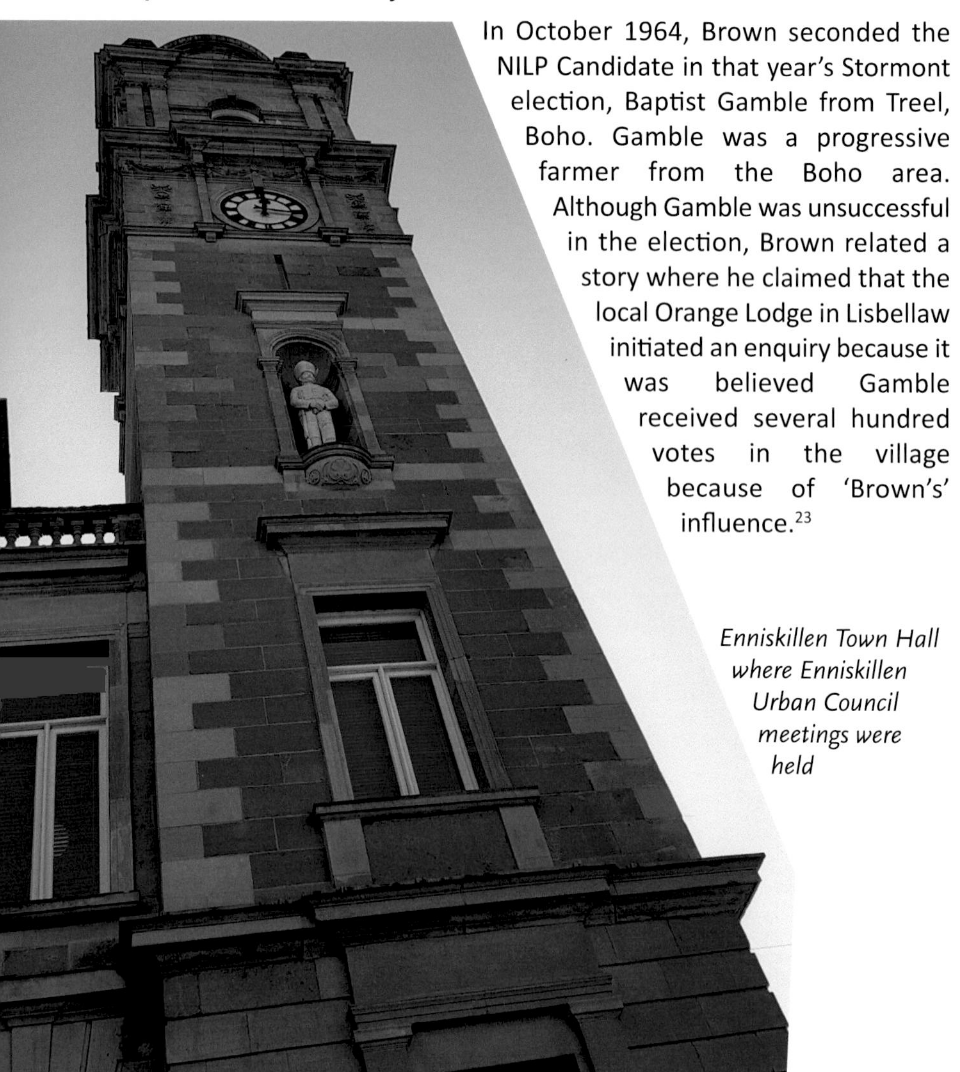

Enniskillen Town Hall where Enniskillen Urban Council meetings were held

In May 1965, Taylor Woods a manufacturer of nylons and other clothing products in Enniskillen announced that they were closing their Mill Street plant with the loss of several hundred jobs. Although there had been allegations of sectarianism and religious discrimination in the company, it was a major blow to the local economy. Brown was extremely critical of the stewardship of Government funding in the plant which he believed had been wasted on perks for the company executives. He asserted the belief, often repeated since, that the Government were trying to turn Fermanagh into 'a sanctuary for the idle rich'.[24] In June 1965, when the future of the Ulster Transport Authority was being debated in the local press, Brown advocated its nationalisation under a Labour Government.[25] At a time when it was claimed that 36% of unemployment in Northern Ireland was in the western area, Brown spoke out at a Fermanagh Trades Union Council (FTUC) meeting criticising the Marquess of Hamilton who had said at a meeting in Florence Court that 'The West is not forgotten'.[26]

By 1968, the Lisbellaw Woollen Mill, which Brown had successfully organised in the early 1950s, had been taken over by the Spamount Woollen Company and was under threat of closure. As the T&G Branch Secretary, Brown led a delegation to meet the Marquess of Hamilton, MP for Fermanagh & South Tyrone, to remind him of his commitments on employment during the previous year's election campaign.[27] They also asked the Marquess to influence his father, the Duke of Abercorn who was a director of the Spamount Woollen company, albeit to no avail. "Brown's agitation" did see several textile companies locating in Fermanagh in later years. Relating the story of the delegation meeting in later years, he said that he told the Marquis that while he, as a socialist, did not vote for him, all the people on the delegation had voted for him in the previous year's election. The Marquis commented that Brown was a very honest man.

In 1968, Brown highlighted an attempt by the owners of the Kent Plastics Factory in Enniskillen to prevent their workers from joining a trade union. The American company had moved into the old Taylor Woods at Derrychara and brought union busting tactics with them from America. Brown got a copy of a letter they had issued to workers and sent it to the *Daily Worker* and the *Belfast Telegraph*. The tactic soon had the desired effect, and the letter was withdrawn by the local management who recognised the unions at the plant. The Fermanagh people were not fooled by the honeyed words of the company President, R.H. Morehouse.[28] The letter said, 'Why not be different? You don't have to belong to a union. I can assure you that your progress and the company's progress will be a lot faster and better if you too are different and unique in not being unionised'.

In September 1966, Brown had supported the Joint Memorandum issued by the Northern Ireland Labour Party (NILP) and the Northern Ireland Committee of the Irish Congress of Trades Unions (NIC-ICTU) which called for,

> Fair representation on public bodies
> An end to discrimination in housing and employment
> Creation of an Ombudsman
> Repeal of the Trades Disputes Act (1927)

The Stormont Government largely ignored their representations. Brown agreed with the aims of the Fermanagh Civil Rights Association (FCRA) founded in 1969 but in the aftermath of what he saw as a take-over by People's Democracy (PD) and more nationalistic elements locally, he stopped attending events as the Civil Rights campaign became overshadowed by violence from the both the State and paramilitaries. The Fermanagh Council of Trades Unions (FCTU) was relaunched in March 1970 with a strong emphasis that it was non-sectarian and non-political. It was determined not to be involved in the sectarian crossfire that was heightened in the Northern Ireland of the 1970s.[29]

By this time, Jim Brown was FCTU Chairperson and had been acting as Chairperson of the Fermanagh Labour Party in 1969[30] when it had met to discuss the political situation which he later described as a 'Thieves' Quarrel'.[31] Attending a PD meeting in Enniskillen Town Hall attended by 400 people, Brown said 'the whole political setup was a thieves' quarrel. The big question was not whether one wanted to go to heaven via Rome or Paisley but how to achieve something better for us and our children'.

In November 1971, along with Unipork Convenor Brendan Heuston from Lisnaskea and T&G full-time Official George Johnston, Brown met with Harry West, then Minister for Agriculture and Private Secretary to the

Minister for Commerce Robin Bailie, to lobby for more investment in response to growing unemployment in Fermanagh.[32]

In 1974, Brown took a strong stance against the Ulster Worker's Council (UWC) Strike which took place between Wednesday 15 May 1974 and Tuesday 28 May 1974.[33] It was called by Unionists in protest at the political and security situation in Northern Ireland and more particularly at the proposals in the Sunningdale Agreement which would have given the Government of the Republic of Ireland a direct say in the running of the province. The strike lasted two weeks and succeeded in bringing down the power-sharing Northern Ireland Executive. Responsibility for the Government of Northern Ireland then reverted to the British Parliament at Westminster under the arrangements for 'Direct Rule'. Brown speaking to local journalists during an election in October of that year described the UWC Strike as, 'Not a trade union dispute but a completely fascist lockout. I fully support the trade union position and a Bill of Rights for Northern Ireland'.[34] Brown kept this position throughout the conflict and refused to allow his union activities to be diverted down any sectarian blind alleyways.

Industrial Struggles

In 1978 Brown along with Brendan Heuston, the T&G Branch Chair and Convenor in the Unipork factory, came to the defence of a group of young workers in the village of Derrygonnelly, a small village about fourteen miles from Enniskillen which dates from the 1830s. Located in the west of the county, it has a population of just under a thousand people. Young workers in a small company there, Fermanagh Wood Products, were looking for a wage increase and union recognition. A nasty dispute ensued when pickets were stoned by local troublemakers. The young people and their parents were also pressurised to return to work by a local priest. The dispute ended when, against the advice of their union, the young people out of frustration occupied the factory and were removed by the Royal Ulster Constabulary (RUC).[35]

At the opening of 1979, Brown was cited in the local papers calling for support for local health workers who were threatening strike action. By October, he was standing on the picket line with local workers in the GT Exhaust factory on the Irvinestown road. The factory was owned by Gilbert

Tunney, a well-known anti-trade union employer.[36] Tunney's brother Hugh owned a meat factory further down the Irvinestown Road and fell afoul of the Dublin dockers when he tried to break a strike and the union at that meat plant.

By August 1978, 2,000 people had died in the Troubles and amongst the many outrages in Fermanagh was an attack on Council workers whose van was riddled with gunfire leading to the death of one worker, Patrick Fee, and the serious injury of several others. Brown and the FCTU strongly condemned the attack, telling the gunmen to 'get off our back'.[37] Sadly, this was not to be the last murder of workers in Fermanagh.

The period of 1978-1979, while it witnessed the election of the hated Thatcher Government, was also a significant period in the development of the labour movement in Fermanagh as another generation became active. The ATGWU Branch meeting was organised by Brown on the first Thursday of every month, religiously at 7.30pm in various locations in Enniskillen. It is now held in Fermanagh House, a community facility located at Broadmeadow Place, Enniskillen. Brown also held a clinic in the Royal Hotel on Saturday nights from 7pm.

I was encouraged to attend the clinic when I joined the union in late 1978 by Tommy Campbell, who had also recently joined the union and became Shop Steward for Enterprise Ulster in Fermanagh. Enterprise Ulster was an employment scheme which carried out some excellent work in providing playgrounds and river walks in the county during the 1970s and early 1980s at a time of chronic unemployment. I had become active when the late Leo Monaghan encouraged me to get involved after organising the union in Peeter's Picture Frames, Chanter Hill, Enniskillen where we both worked in 1978.

The clinic was a great opportunity for members and Shop Stewards to meet Brown informally and work out tactics to deal with problems at work between Branch meetings. Whenever us younger inexperienced representatives got frustrated with a particularly thorny issue, Jim would say, 'Don't worry lads, we'll get them in the long grass'. A second benefit of the clinics was when union business was done and, afterwards over a beer, discussion inevitably drifted to local politics.

Brown, although much more knowledgeable and experienced than us comparative youngsters and a member of the Communist Party of Ireland

(CPI) from the 1950s, never pushed his politics on you. Instead, he posed questions which made you think more about politics and the society we lived in. The result was that even more questions were posed in the weeks and months following as we developed as trade union and political activists.

Two other local activists Séamus Murphy and John Jones were also involved in the same discussions at various stages. Jones's grandfather, also John, had been a founder member of the T&G Branch and its first Secretary. Some within the group became CPI members or joined the Workers' Party or the Labour and Trade Union Group. Others did not align with any socialist or communist groupings. The group was a very broad gathering of active trade unionists over the years which made a significant contribution to the development of trade unionism and class politics in the county. In later years, Brown described myself, Tommy Campbell and Davy Kettyles as 'The Three Cubs'.

A New Generation

This period witnessed the resurgence of the FCTU. Tommy Campbell was elected as Secretary with Brown as Chair and myself as a T&G delegate along with a few other branch members. One of the biggest trade union demonstrations in Fermanagh occurred on 2 April 1980. Brown as FCTU Chair addressed the rally in Enniskillen's Diamond with Tommy Campbell and John Freeman, T&G Irish Regional Secretary. Brown attacked the Tories and their supporters for making savage cut-backs in public services and also took aim at a local Councillor from the Irish Independence Party, Patrick McCaffrey, who had clashed with Tommy Campbell in the local press because of his criticism of the local Council. A series of letters were exchanged in the press for some weeks during which

March and demonstration from the Gaol Square to the Diamond, Enniskillen, 2 April 1980: l-r Tommy Campbell, Jim Brown, Davy Kettyles, Jim Quinn, John Freeman (ATGWU Regional Secretary) & Leo Monaghan.

McCaffrey accused Brown of being a 'Pink Unionist'. Brown refuted this charge in later editions and labelled Councillor Mc Caffrey as a 'Green crested Tory'. The letters pages of local papers were then a well-used conduit for political discussion.

1981 was a difficult period for everyone. People were being murdered on an almost daily basis and the second Hunger Strike began on 1 March. The tension came close to Brown when one of his neighbours in Lisbellaw was intimidated from their home because of their religion. Brown did not hesitate to condemn the intimidation publicly and called for it to end.[38] A story is told about the Twelfth of July County Demonstration by the Orange Order being held in Lisbellaw and extra policing being drafted in from Belfast to protect the event because of the security situation. Brown was told of a conversation between a local policeman and his Belfast colleague who had noticed there was no flag hanging from Brown's house. He said, 'Is that a Catholic family living there?' His local colleague responded, 'That boy is far worse than that, he's a communist'. The story provides an insight as to how Brown was regarded amongst the different sections of the Lisbellaw community.

In the May General Election, hunger striker Bobby Sands was elected Westminster MP for Fermanagh & South Tyrone.[39] For the Council election in May – and against the tide – local trade union and Labour activists formed a new group called the Fermanagh Labour League and ran Tommy Campbell as a candidate to challenge both Unionists and Nationalists for a seat in Enniskillen. Brown as usual supported the campaign and for his efforts had his car attacked during a canvas in the mainly Unionist estate of Derrychara. The campaign was also not welcomed by the Irish Independence Party whose supporters tore down every Labour poster erected in the Enniskillen area. In the event, Campbell was not elected but he did lay the ground for a victory six years later in 1987 for Davy Kettyles who was proposed by Brown for the seat.

Brown was the first Representative from Region 11 (Ireland) to the T&G's National Agricultural and Allied Workers Trade Group in 1983/1984. He joined at a time when it had the job of steering the Trade Group through a difficult period of transformation following the merger of the National Union of Agricultural & Allied Workers (NUAAW) with the T&G in 1983.[40] While a member of this Trade Group, Brown met the Labour MP Joan

Posters for Fermanagh Labour League Candidate Tommy Campbell on the hoarding around Enniskillen Courthouse, May 1981 Council elections.

Maynard.[41] Along with other left members of the Trade Group, he would meet her in the House of Commons prior to their National Trade Group Meetings. She was among a select group of working-class women to be elected to Westminster. The daughter of a farmer in North Yorkshire, she attended the village school at Ampleforth until she was fourteen, when her formal education ended. After the war, Maynard got involved in politics. Until 1945 the rule of the squirearchy was unchallenged in North Yorkshire so Maynard became a founder member of the Thirsk Labour Party, chosen by default as Secretary and, later, as Labour Agent for Thirsk and Malton. By the time she stepped down, the Constituency Labour Party, despite being in a Tory stronghold, had more than 2,000 members, one of the largest in the country.

In 1958, Maynard stood for the County Council, defeating first the local chemist, then the parson and finally the squire himself, thereby demonstrating – long before New Labour was ever heard of – that it was possible for a socialist to be elected deep behind enemy lines, without having to hide her or his views under a bushel. She was active in the NUAAW and played a leading part in ending the tied-cottage system that caused misery for many rural workers and their families.[42] Brown had a great respect for Maynard who had a similar background to himself.

Throughout the years, Brown made his views known on a range of issues from the exploitation of Action for Community Employment (ACE) scheme workers in the development of the Council-owned Marble Arch Caves Development,[43] to supporting the National Union of Mineworkers and others in their struggle for jobs and justice.[44] In April 1985, Brown welcomed the Conference of the Irish Congress of Trades Unions, Northern Ireland Committee (NIC-ICTU) to Fermanagh for the first time. The conference was held in the Lakeland Forum.[45] It was addressed by Inez Mc Cormack as the first woman Chair of the NIC-ICTU.[46]

Brown did not escape the sectarian attacks and during the Anglo-Irish Agreement protests in the 1980s, when he refused to stop at an illegal roadblock on Enniskillen's Dublin Road when on his way to work, his car was damaged. That night graffiti was painted on the garages beside his home saying, 'Brown is a Communist Bastard'. Commenting on the slogan, Brown said the first part was true but the slogan writers would have to ask his mother about the second part. Interestingly the good people of Lisbellaw made sure the slogan was removed within twenty-four hours.

Andy Barr, Jim Brown, Brendan Heuston, George Johnston, Andy Holmes and Tommy Campbell outside 1985 NIC-ICTU Conference in the Lakeland Forum

Brown's campaigning continued throughout the 1980s. He supported the striking print workers at Wapping, condemned the imposition of twelve-hour shifts in the local health service and supported the local campaign to boycott South African goods in local shops as part of the struggle against Apartheid in South Africa.[47] In early 1989, he was again back in the papers condemning the privatisation of the canteen facilities in the local Council-run leisure centre, the Lakeland Forum. [48]

Community Development

During the 1980s, Brown became involved in local community development and in particular the Enniskillen Welfare Rights Unit, a project of the Enniskillen Community Development Project (ECDP). Brown had been a member of the Social Security Appeal Tribunals for many years and instructed several of us as to how to represent cases for our members and their families at the tribunals. Brown became a member of the ECDP's Committee and later its Chair. In August 1989, when reviewing the progress of the ECDP as Chair, he reported that in the previous five years its advice centre had dealt with 10,000 cases and raised more than £1,500,000 for claimants in the Fermanagh Community.[49]

The Remembrance Day Bomb

The Remembrance Day bomb on 8 November 1987 in Enniskillen visited a dreadful atrocity upon the Fermanagh Community. One of the victims was a member of the local ATGWU Branch, Bertha Armstrong, who was murdered along with her husband Wesley. The Branch expressed its horror and sadness in a statement issued to the local papers in the aftermath.[50] Brown along with the first woman Secretary of the FCTU, the late Rosemary Stennett, also issued a hard-hitting statement at Christmas of 1987 condemning all violence:[51]

> 'There are no justifications, no legitimate targets, no acceptable levels of violence and workers who in any way, assist, promote or contribute financially to those who threaten these rights are, in reality threatening their fellow workers, their trade union colleagues and their livelihood.'[52]

Throughout the early 1990s, Brown continued to campaign around a range of local issues including, Support for Ambulance Workers, Pension Rights,

Further Education Lecturers, the Maternity Action Committee, retention of the Unipork factory and opposed the exploitation of Young People on Youth Training Schemes. His energy and commitment were unbounded and inspired and energised those around him.

T&G Gold medal awarded to Jim Brown, 1990

Honours

In June 1990 Brown's service to the union movement from 1946 and the T&G was honoured at a ceremony in the Railway Hotel in Enniskillen. Earlier in the year Brown was presented with the T&G Gold Medal by Ron Todd, General Secretary of the union at its Biennial Delegate Conference in Blackpool in 1991.[53] Brown's service to the union to that point made impressive reading:

> Branch Secretary, 1948-1990,
>
> Regional Committee Member, 1962-1989
>
> General Workers National Trade Group, 1973-1983
>
> Agricultural Trade Group, 1983-1989
>
> Fermanagh Trades Union Council,1960-1990
>
> Member of the Local Appeal Tribunals, Erne Youth & Community Workshop Committee, Enniskillen Community Development Project and Unemployed Resource Centre.

Th inscription on the Gold Medal read: 'Presented to Bro. J. Brown, No. 11/41 Branch, in appreciation of his loyal and devoted service to the union (1945-1990)'.

Regional Secretary John Freeman nicely summed up Brown's contribution when he said, 'When courage was needed, Jim was always in the fore front'.[54] Brown himself, of course, had the last word and emphasised he was only retiring from work and the Regional Committee 'but not the struggle[55]. Freeman presented Brown with 'The Slate Man' service award, the inscription reading 'Presented by the Irish Regional Committee to Bro. Jimmy Brown, 11/41 Branch ATGWU, in appreciation of his services to the Union'.

Locally, a framed presentation was made to Brown and his wife Margaret on 11 May 1990. It bore the logo of the ATGWU and the inscription read, 'Amalgamated Transport & General Workers' Union (Fermanagh) - Fermanagh Trade Unionists - presented to Jim Brown in recognition of his outstanding service to the working class of Fermanagh. The presentation party included George Johnston, T&G Officer; Brendan Heuston (Unipork Convenor & Branch Chair); Jim Quinn (3/41 Branch); Seán Morrissey (retired Regional Education Officer); and Úna Owens (Local Authority Steward).

Above: TGWU Slate Man awarded to Jim Brown, 1990

Left: Presentation to Jim Brown in May 1998 on his retirement: back, l-r, George Johnston (Local District TGWU Official), Brendan Heuston (TGWU Convenor Uni-Pork and Branch Chair), Jim Quinn (Development Officer, Counteract, ICTU Anti- Intimidation Unit): front, l-r Seán Morrisey (Retired Regional Education Officer), Jim Brown, Margaret Brown, Una Owens (Shop Steward, Local Authority, Lakeland Forum).

The Struggle for Peace

As political talks aimed at ending the conflict in Northern Ireland stumbled along in the 1990s, sectarian violence and attacks on workers continued unabated. Brown addressed major demonstrations of workers in Enniskillen in 1993 and again in 1996 condemning the violence.[56] In July 1997, Brown again clashed with an Ulster Unionist Councillor who had publicly advocated running Travellers out of the county with a shotgun. Brown called upon the authorities to prosecute the Councillor concerned and while that did not happen, the statement has never been repeated publicly in the county since then.[57]

At a rally in Enniskillen in February 1998, held as political dialogue increased, Brown called for political talks to continue and in May urged a 'Yes' vote in the Good Friday referendum. Later in May, he took part in a local dialogue around the Yes Campaign with David Ervine of the Progressive Unionist Party (PUP)[58] and Monica McWilliams, of the Northern Ireland Women's Coalition (NIWC).[59]

Jim Brown with TGWU General Secretary Bill Morris in Enniskillen Town Hall June 1998 with the late Leo Monaghan, Shop Steward in Peeter's Picture Frames, who got the author involved in the union in 1978.

In 1998, May was a particularly busy month for Brown as he welcomed Bill Morris to a Civic Reception in Enniskillen Town Hall.[60] Morris was the first T&G General Secretary to visit Fermanagh, the occasion being a celebration of the 75th Anniversary of the founding of the Enniskillen ATGWU Branch. Brown took that opportunity to call upon people to support the candidates from the NIWC in the election for the new Assembly. On 15 August 1998, the terrible Omagh bomb brought bloody devastation to the community. Brown's message in the local media condemned the dissidents who ignored the massive vote for Peace. He urged that the best way to honour the Omagh dead was to 'Build Peace Across Our Land'.[61]

Brown remained energetically involved with his union and local community up to his death. One of his last public acts was to open a new

TGWU District Offices, Enniskillen

T&G District Centre in Enniskillen in 2001. He marvelled at the progress made from his first involvement in the 1940s when it was nearly impossible to get a room for a union meeting in Enniskillen let alone an office.[62]

Death and Legacy

On 17 June 2003, while leaving a meeting in Dublin, I received the sad news that my comrade and friend, Jim Brown had passed away. He left behind Margaret, his soul mate and rock. Margaret herself died on 26 October 2008 having never got over her husband's death. Her brother John had passed a few years before. Brown had asked me many years before his death to do the oration at his funeral. Although not a practising Christian, he was buried out of his wife Margaret's Methodist Church in Lisbellaw. With the kind permission of the visiting Minister, Reverend Kingston, his comrades were able to give Jim the send-off he asked for.

Local Trade Unionists laying a wreath on Mayday at the grave of Jim Brown, Tattygare Church Yard, Lisbellaw: l-r, Derek Parton, Austin Mc Quaid, Séamus Murphy & Jim Quinn

Brown followed in the footsteps of other radicals from Fermanagh's Protestant community such as William Scott from Letterbreen who moved to Dublin in the early 1900s and was a member of the Irish Citizen Army during the 1913 Dublin Lockout led by William Martin Murphy, owner of the *Irish Independent*.[63] Scott's son, Bill was one of the first Irishmen to travel to Spain to defend the Republic against fascist attack.[64]

Since Brown's passing local trade unionists have laid a wreath on his grave and made a short oration at Tattygare Graveyard each year around May Day. In 2022, a new Workers' Memorial was installed in the Brook Park, Enniskillen, which includes an inscription in Brown's memory: 'Jim Brown, Chairperson FCTU, trade unionist, socialist, anti-fascist, 1925-2003'. In addition, there is a commemorative bench to him in the park and in future it is planned that the annual May Day tribute will be made there. Unite the Union in Ireland have organised political schools in the form of lectures and discussions for several years in the Belfast Regional Office in memory of Jim Brown organised by Greg Sachno, Regional Education Officer, a friend and admirer of Brown.

Fermanagh workers will ensure that the legacy of Jim Brown will be maintained and that they will continue to 'get them in the long grass'. Ní bheidh a leithéid ann arís - There will not be his likes again.

Andrew Cathers, Chair FCTU, at the unveiling in Brook Park in April 2022 of the Workers' Memorial, The panel on the lower left of the memorial remembers Jim Brown

UNITE POLITICAL SUMMER SCHOOL 2011

Tuesday, August 9, 1pm, Unite office, Antrim Road, Belfast

THIS MACHINE

It Kills Fascists

THE FIRST JIM BROWN DEBATE

KEYNOTE SPEAKER:
DEREK WALL
ENVIRONMENTAL ACTIVIST AND
MORNING STAR CONTRIBUTOR
'THE GREEN LEFT ALTERNATIVES'
OPENING REMARKS:
JIMMY QUINN,
UNITE SENIOR ORGANISER
CHAIR:
RITCHIE BROWNE,
UNITE IRELAND EDUCATION OFFICER

Jim Brown (front left)

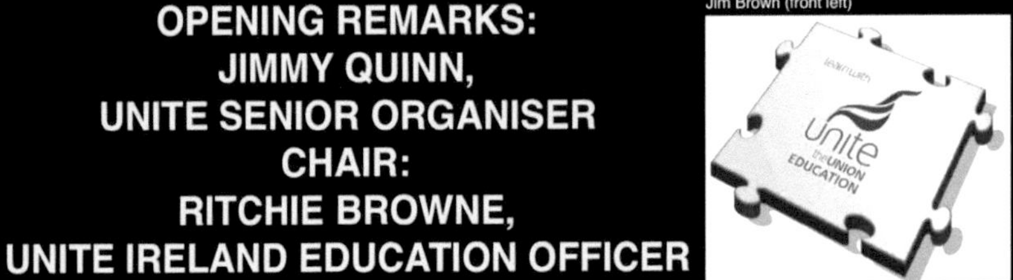

Appendix 1:

A Delightful Subversive

Smiling eyes shine their light on a life
full of struggle and strife.
No Leprechauns or fairy tales in his book
just stories that stretched our minds
and lifted us from our behinds
to stand tall with him
as he looked us straight in the eye
that Giant born from amongst
the real little people.

A tribute to Jimmy Brown who introduced me to the trade union and labour movement in Fermanagh and beyond. The description of a 'Delightful Subversive' comes from Marian Hyndman, the author of a book about protestant workers in Northern Ireland, who interviewed Jim about his life and struggles in rural Fermanagh.

Thomas Campbell
UNITE the Union, Retired Regional Organiser

Appendix 2:

Jim Quinn's Oration For Jim Brown, Lisbellaw Methodist Church, 20 June 2003

Ladies and Gentlemen, Minister, Sisters and Brothers, Comrades and Friends

May I firstly on behalf of my union, the Transport & General Workers' Union, and the trade union movement in Ireland and Britain express our deepest condolences to Jim's wife, Margaret, and the family circle at this sad time. We know you were behind Jim in everything he done, and we thank you for helping him to make such a huge contribution to our Movement.

It is a rare privilege for any of us to meet someone great in our lives let alone to have them as a friend and comrade. Jim Brown was such a person. I met Jim nearly twenty-five years ago when I became a member of the union he loved so much, the Transport & General Workers' Union. At that time Jim had already been a member for more than twenty-five years. I can well remember him cajoling us, encouraging us, supporting us, explaining to us about the need to be organised to protect the interests of working-class people.

Jim knew what had to be done. He had struggled all his life against the evils of exploitation, poverty, unemployment, war, sectarianism, and racism. Jim knew about the evils of the hiring system. He knew about the evils of fascism and Nazism and went to fight the fascist monster in the deserts of North Africa and at Dunkirk. He was commended for his bravery after being wounded twice in action.

But his proudest moment was when he received the Gold Medal of the Transport & General Workers' Union after fifty years of active membership. Jim's struggle did not end when the Second World War ended. During the war Jim had learnt about socialism and trade unionism from his commanding officer, a Lieutenant Sinclair from Aberdeen.

After being demobbed in Bristol he joined with the legendary Belfast socialist Betty Sinclair selling the *Daily Worker* on the streets of that city. Indeed, only last week he dropped several copies of its successor, the *Morning Star*, on to my desk with the comment, 'Take a look at the article on page four, lad, what do you think of that?'

Jim agitated and organised everywhere that privilege and power tried to exploit the underdog. Whether on the Agricultural Wage Committees or the Social Security Tribunals, whether across a negotiating table or at the street meeting, Jim Brown was a tower of strength for those afraid to speak up for themselves. I remember him telling the story of going into a meeting with a nervous companion who said, 'Now, Jim, don't be rocking the boat too hard in here' to which Jim replied, 'Don't worry, son, I won't rock the boat, I'll turn it right over!'

That was Jim Brown, never afraid to court controversy in the cause of right. But Jim also tried to unite people and chaired the umbrella body for unions, the Fermanagh Council of Trade Unions in the county for many years. Likewise, while his politics were more left wing than the Northern Ireland Labour Party, he nevertheless supported its activities in the county during the 1960s. That was why when the Civil Rights movement came into being in the late 1960s, Jim lent it his support until bigotry and violence engulfed our society. Jim detested the violence, sectarianism and oppression which destroyed so many lives in our community. He could never accept why our communities could not unite to fight for a better life instead of fighting each other.

Nor did Jim confine his activities to Fermanagh. He was known throughout the island of Ireland and in England, Scotland, and Wales for his trade union work. I remember him telling me about being threatened with deportation from the Republic of Ireland by a large Garda because he used a bicycle to block a bridge during an unemployed protest. Similarly, I recall him making a passionate speech about unemployment in Belfast when the Chair said, 'Your out of time, Jim, I'm going to switch off your microphone'. Jim replied, 'Switch me off if you like but I'm finishing what I started' and his voice continued to boom across the conference hall to rapturous applause without the support of a microphone.

That was Jim Brown, a man they could not silence. Even now Jim is not silent because he has left a legacy in this county, in Northern Ireland and beyond which will carry on his work for Peace, Work and Progress and against Violence, Prejudice and Poverty.

Jim was proud that his work had created two union Officials and a socialist Councillor not to mention hundreds of union and community activists in the county too many to name. Jim was proud of the work of the Welfare Rights Unit and Community Training Services in Enniskillen, of which he was Chair for many years. He was even prouder when his union opened a new office in Enniskillen a few years ago.

Jim Brown, our comrade and friend, left a legacy which we can be proud of. For as long as we pursue that legacy, Jim Brown will live in our hearts and our struggles. If he were here, Jim would say in the immortal words of Joe Hill, 'Don't mourn, Organise!'

Farewell Comrade Jim. It has been a privilege to be your friend.

Jim Quinn

Jim Browne Memorial Banner at Belfast May Day Parade

Bibliography

Primary Sources

Irish Genealogy Archive, www.irishgenealogy.ie/en/

Irish Newspaper Archives, www.irishnewsarchive.com

Newspapers & Journals

Belfast Telegraph

Fermanagh Herald

Guardian

Impartial Reporter

Published Sources

Blair, May. *Hiring Fairs and Market Places*, (Appletree Press, Belfast, 2007)

Cody, Séamus; O'Dowd, John; and Rigney, Peter. *The Parliament of Labour, 100 Years of the Dublin Council of Trade Unions*, (Dublin Council of Trade Unions, Dublin, 1986)

Hyndman, Marilyn. *Further Afield, Journeys from a Protestant Past*, (Beyond the Pale Publications, Belfast, 1996)

Livingstone, Patrick. *The Fermanagh Story*, (Cumann Seanchais, Chlocair, Enniskillen, 1969)

Maguire, Dermot. *The Fermanagh Civil Rights Campaign in its Wider Context, 1969-1974,* (Fermanagh, 2023)

O'Connor, Emmet. *A Labour History of Ireland, 1824-2000*, (University College Dublin Press, Dublin, 2011)

Wynn, Bob. *The History of the Farmworkers Union, 1947-1984*, (TGWU, London, 1993)

Notes

Note that all internet sources were retrieved on 18 September 2023.

1 The *Annals of Ulster* are the story of medieval Ireland from 431 to 1540, see https://celt.ucc.ie/published/T100001A/index.html/
2 Peadar Livingstone, *The Fermanagh Story*, (Cumann Seanchais Chlochair, Enniskillen, 1969), p. 206.
3 Marilyn Hyndman, *Further Afield, Journeys from a Protestant Past*, (Beyond the Pale Publications, Belfast, 1996), pp. 148-153
4 Paris buns are sweetened breadlike cakes similar to a scone or rock cake and appear to be of Scots origin.
5 May Blair, *Hiring Fairs and Market Places*, (Appletree Press, Belfast, 2007), pp. 110-129.
6 'Things – 75 years ago', *Impartial Reporter,* 14 September 1989.
7 Bryan MacMahon, *Robert Tressell, Dubliner: Author of The Ragged Trousered Philanthropists*, (Kilmacud Stillorgan Local History Society, Dublin, 2014).
8 For full text see, www.marxists.org/archive/marx/works/download/pdf/Manifesto.pdf.
9 Born in Hooker Street, Belfast, Sinclair was a mill worker and joined the Revolutionary Workers' Groups in 1932 and attended the Lenin School in Moscow in 1935. She was full-time Secretary of Belfast Trades Council, 1947-1975, and Chair, Northern Ireland Civil Rights Association, 1967-1969. See, Hazel Morrissey, 'Betty Sinclair: a woman's fight for socialism, 1910-1981, *Saothar 9*, 1983, pp. 121-132; Maurice Cronin, 'Sinclair, Elizabeth (Betty)', Dictionary of Irish Biography, https://dib.cambridge.org/viewReadPage.do?articleId=a8088.
10 The title ATGWU was to distinguish it from the Dublin-based Irish Transport & General Workers' Union founded in 1909. For details, see Matt Merrigan, *Eagle or Cuckoo? The Story of the ATGWU in Ireland*, (Matmer Publications, Dubin, 1989).
11 *Fermanagh Herald*, 9 June 1990.
12 Emmet O'Connor, *A Labour History of Ireland, 1824-2000*, (University College, Dublin Press 2011) p. 181. Agnew, 1878-1958, had Labourite politics and often clashed with conservative Nationalist politicians. He formed the Armagh Employed & Unemployed Association in 1932 and formed a NILP Branch in 1933 and the Armagh Federation of Labour in 1937. He held the Stormont seat for South Armagh for the NILP from 1938-1945 and remained a local council representative until 1958.
13 *Fermanagh Herald*, 20 February 1943.
14 *Fermanagh Herald*, 20 March 1954.
15 *Fermanagh Herald*, 9 June 1951.

16 O'Connor, *A Labour History of Ireland, op. cit*., p. 197. Hugh Downey (Belfast Dock) and Robert Getgood (Belfast Oldpark) won seats in 1945.
17 See Evanne Kilmurray, *Fight, Starve or Emigrate: A History of the Unemployed Associations in the 1950s*, (Larkin Unemployed Centre, Dublin, 1988), available online at www.leftarchive.ie/document/view/6349/, and Séamus Cody, John O'Dowd & Peter Rigney, *The Parliament of Labour, 100 Years of the Dublin Council of Trade Unions*, (Dublin Council of Trade Unions, Dublin, 1986), p. 200.
18 *Fermanagh Herald*, 19 July 1969. The POEU, formed in 1915, became the National Communications Union in 1985 and, after merging with the Union of Communications Workers in 1995, the Communications Workers' Union (CWU).
19 Dermot Maguire, *The Fermanagh Civil Rights Campaign in Its Wider Context, 1969-1974*, (Enniskillen, 2023), p. 64.
20 *Fermanagh Herald*, 3 March 1979.
21 *Fermanagh Herald*, 8 February 1964.
22 *Fermanagh Herald*, 11 April 1959.
23 On 15 October 1964, the seat was won by James Marquess Hamilton (Unionist), 30,690; Aloysius Molloy (Independent Republican), 16,138; Giles FitzHerbert (Ulster Liberal), 6,006; and Gamble, 2,339.
24 *Fermanagh Herald*, 22 May 1965.
25 *Fermanagh Herald*, 12 June 1965.
26 *Fermanagh Herald*, 6 November 1965.
27 *Fermanagh Herald*, 6 April 1968.
28 *Belfast Telegraph*, 31 August 1968.
29 *Fermanagh Herald*, 11 April 1970.
30 *Impartial Reporter*, 6 February 1969.
31 *Fermanagh Herald*, 22 February 1969.
32 *Fermanagh Herald*, 11 December 1971.
33 For details see Don Anderson, *Fourteen Days in May*, (Gill & Macmillan, Dublin, 1994) and Robert Fisk, *Point of No Return: The Strike Which Broke British Rule in Ulster*, (Harper Collins, London, 1975).
34 *Fermanagh Herald*, 5 October 1974.
35 *Fermanagh Herald*, 30 September 1978.
36 *Fermanagh Herald*, 6 October 1979.
37 *Fermanagh Herald*, 2 August 1978.
38 *Fermanagh Herald*, 18 July 1981.
39 Sands, born in Dunmurry in 1954, was apprenticed as a coachbuilder in Newtownabbey until driven from employment by sectarian intimidation. He became a barman and joined the Provisional IRA. Leader of the IRA prisoners in the Maze, he began a Hunger Strike on 1 March 1981 and died on 5 May.

On 9 April 1981, Sands, standing as an Anti H-Block candidate, polled 30,493 votes to defeat Ulster Unionist Harry West, 29,046.

40 Bob Wynn, *Skilled at all Trades, The History of the Farmworkers' Union, 1947-1984*, (TGWU, London, 1993).

41 Maynard, 1921-1998, was born in Easingwold, North Yorkshire, became NUAAW Vice President and campaigned throughout her life for rural workers and their families. She was Labour MP for Sheffield Brightside, 1974-1987, and was active in the left-wing Campaign Group and the Troops Out Movement.

42 Maynard's obituary by Chris Mullin, MP, *Guardian*, 23 September 2011.

43 *Fermanagh Herald*, 24 December 1983.

44 *Fermanagh Herald*, 29 December 1984.

45 *Fermanagh Herald*, 27 April 1985.

46 For discussion of McCormack's outstanding contribution, see Francis Devine, 'Inez McCormack: changing everything, 1943-2013' in Francis Devine & Kieran Jack McGinley (eds), *Left Lives in Twentieth Century Ireland*, (Umiskin Press, Dublin, 2017), pp 211-234; Theresa Moriarty, 'Inez McCormack', *Saothar 38*, 2013, pp. 184-185; and Margaret Ward, 'Inez McCormack: challenging inequalities in Northern Ireland' in John Cunningham, Francis Devine & Sonja Tiernan, *Labour History in Irish History*, (ILHS/Umiskin Press, Dublin, 2023), pp. 360-376.

47 *Fermanagh Herald*, 27 August 1988.

48 *Fermanagh Herald*, 18 February 1989.

49 *Fermanagh Herald*, 19 August 1989.

50 *Fermanagh Herald*, 5 December 1987.

51 Stennett was a school cook and ATGWU member. She died on 23 July 2015.

52 *Fermanagh Herald*, 9 January 1988.

53 Ron Todd, born in Walthamstow, London in 1927, rose to prominence as a TGWU Convenor in Ford's, Dagenham, becoming a full-time Official in Edmonton and Stratford in 1975 and National Organiser, 1978. He had expected this latter position to be his last before retiring from the union but the untimely death of General Secretary Moss Evans saw him elected to succeed him in 1985, serving until 1992. Todd died in 2005.

54 Freeman, born in Oldpark, north Belfast in 1933, worked in Short & Harland after returning from Australia in 1962 and became ATGWU Convenor and gained election to the Union's Executive. From 1974-1998, he was Irish Regional Secretary, serving as ICTU President, 1995-1997. He faced intimidation from the Loyalist Association of Workers for his opposition to Internment. He died in 1998. See Peter Collins, 'John Freeman: a life on the left', *Saothar 24*, 1999, pp. 129-138.

55 *Fermanagh Herald*, 9 June 1990.

56 *Fermanagh Herald*, 20 November 1993, 21 February 1996.
57 *Fermanagh Herald*, 16 July 1997.
58 David Ervine, 1953-2007, was jailed for his UVF activities and served as a PUP MLA for Belfast East, 1998-2007.
59 Monica McWilliams, born in Ballymoney in 1954, was a co-founder of the NIWC in 1996 and was elected as a delegate at the Multi-Party Peace Negotiations which led to the Goood Friday Agreement. From 1998-2003, she served as MLA for Belfast South and chaired the Implementation Committee on Human Rights on behalf of the British and Irish Governments. She was Chief Commissioner of the Northern Ireland Human Rights Commission, 2005–2011, and was the Oversight Commissioner for Prison Reform in Northern Ireland, 2011–2015. Emeritus Professor in the Transitional Justice Institute at Ulster University Professor of at the University of Ulster, she sits on the Independent Reporting Commission for the disbandment of paramilitary organisations.
60 Morris was born in Jamaica in 1935 and elected to the TGWU Executive in 1972 before being appointed to various District Officer posts. In 1979, he became National Secretary Passenger Services and Deputy General Secretary, 1985. In 1992 he was elected General Sectary. He was knighted on his retirement in 2003 and became Baron Morris of Handsworth in 2008.
61 *Fermanagh Herald*, 26 August 1998.
62 *Fermanagh Herald*, 4 April 2001.
63 William John Scott was born to a Church of Ireland family in Letterbreen in 1876. After completing his apprenticeship as a bricklayer, he and his wife Mary moved to Dublin where he became active in his union and joined the ICA. In 1916, he saw action in St Stephen's Green. He was not imprisoned after the Rising and he and his eldest son Alexander joined F Company, 4th Battalion, Dublin Brigade and fought in the War of Independence and on the anti-Treaty side in the Civil War. He died on 24 December 1947.
64 William 'Bill' Scott, 1908-1980, came from Ring Street, Dublin, and was active in the CPI. In Spain, he was elected Political Commissar for the English Tom Mann Centuria in September 1936, before joining with the German Thaelmann Battalion in the defence of Madrid. He returned to activity in the Bricklayer's Union and the CPI.

Fermanagh Labour League poster
for Tommy Campbell

Jim Quinn addresses a meteting

Jim Brown at Labour Party Dinner in the Melvin House, Enniskillen, 1964

Liam McBrinn, then ATGWU Education Officer with Jim Brown in the newly-opened T&G Enniskillen District Office in 2002

Jim Brown's Welfare Unit caravan strategically placed between the Dole Office and Housing Executive

Jim Brown & Terry Carlin, ICTU Northern Ireland Officer at a protest in Enniskillen against unemployment in November 1982